ANGEL GIRL

story by **Laurie Friedman**

illustrations by **Ofra Amit**

Based on a true story

CAROLRHODA BOOKS   MINNEAPOLIS · NEW YORK

To Herman and Roma Rosenblat . . . for sharing your story with me.

And special thanks to my father-in-law, Lenny Friedman, who brought it to my attention.

With love and gratitude,

—L.B.F.

To Herman and Roma

—O.A.

Text copyright © 2008 by Laurie B. Friedman
Illustrations copyright © 2008 by Ofra Amit

Carolrhoda Books
A division of Lerner Publishing Group, Inc.
241 First Avenue North
Minneapolis, MN 55401 U.S.A.

Website address: www.lernerbooks.com

The photographs on page 32 appear courtesy of Herman and Roma Rosenblat.

Library of Congress Cataloging-in-Publication Data

Friedman, Laurie B.
    Angel girl / by Laurie Friedman ; illustrations by Ofra Amit.
        p.   cm.
    ISBN 978—0—8225—8739—2 (lib. bdg. : alk. paper)
    1. Rosenblat, Herman. 2. Jews—Poland—Biography—Juvenile literature. 3. Holocaust,
Jewish (1939—1945)—Poland—Juvenile literature. 4. Jewish children in the Holocaust—Poland
Biography—Juvenile literature. 5. Friendship in literature—Juvenile literature. I. Amit, Ofra.
II. Title.
    DS134.72.R67F75 2008
    940.53'18092—dc22 [B]   2007034779

Manufactured in the United States of America
1 2 3 4 5 6 — JR — 13 12 11 10 09 08

Author's Note

Under the best of circumstances, childhood is a happy time when a young person's days are marked by countless hours spent playing, dreaming, learning, discovering, and imagining. Ideally, children grow up surrounded by the warmth and love of family and friends, in the safety of a comfortable place they call home.

But for Jewish children growing up in Europe during World War II (1939–1945), there was no such happiness. For these children, childhood was filled with despair. They were plucked from their homes. They witnessed the murders of their parents and siblings. They were faced with starvation, illness, brutal labor, and death by gas chambers.

During World War II, 1.6 million Jewish children were killed by Adolf Hitler and the Nazis. The numbers are staggering, but the stories behind the numbers are even more painful.

There are as many stories from the war as there were people who were affected by it. Most are very sad. What you are about to read is the story of a real boy named Herman. When I first heard his story, I cried—not because it has such an incredibly sad beginning, but because it has such an unbelievably happy ending.

Laurie Friedman

"Women, children to the right. Men to the left."

Boots clicked. Guns pointed. Commands issued.
Cries floated up and disappeared into the cold morning air like puffs of smoke.

I was tall for my age but still a boy of eleven. I clung to my mother's thin frame.
"Mama, I go with you," I whispered.

She pushed me away to my older brothers, as she walked toward the open train car.
Eyes forward. Body stiff. Head high. "Herman," she said. "The time has come for
you to be a man."

That was the last time I saw my mother.

When it was my turn to go, my train rolled forward.
Carried me away. Hot bodies, hot tears,
squeezed me tight.

My brain filled with words. Mama. Where am I going?
Mama. What am I to do?
Mama. Who will care for me?
Mama . . .

I waited. Waited for her to answer.

When the train stopped, guards grabbed my arms.
Unloaded me into darkness. Gunshots filled the night air.
I was stripped and searched. I was given a uniform
and a work assignment.

"Off to the barracks," shouted a guard.

My feet moved forward. My body filled with fear.
Images swirled around me. My mother cooking dinner.
My father playing the piano. My dog curled up next to me.

I held tight to my brother. "I want to go home."

My brother answered, his voice, thin, flat.
"This is home now."

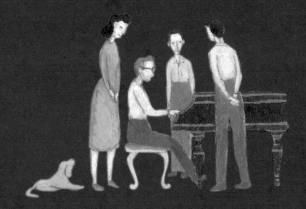

My days at the work camp began at dawn. Lined up. Marched out. No food.
No protection from the cold. Only work. My hands bled. My stomach rumbled.

At first, I tried to pretend.

When I worked in the factory, I imagined myself playing in the park near my home. When I was hungry, I filled myself with the memory of my mother's cooking. When I was cold, I told myself my numb fingertips belonged to someone else.

At night, I was given soup. Soup like water.

I slept on a shelf. My thin body lay pressed amongst hundreds of others.

I thought of things I missed. Little things. A pillow. A toilet. A toothbrush.
Big things. Mama. Always Mama.

"Mama," I asked each night. "When are you coming to tuck me in?" Then I waited.
Cold. Tired. Hungry. Hopeful. Waiting for Mama.

One night, Mama came to me. In a dream. Soft. Certain. Steady.
"Don't worry, Herman." Mama's soft voice soothed me.
"An angel will save you."

Two days later, she appeared. Girl angel. Angel girl. Light.
Luminous. On the other side of the fence.

I moved closer. My angel girl was real.

"You have food?" I whispered.

My angel girl nodded. We watched, waited. One wrong move meant death. My death. Her death.

When the moment was right, she tossed an apple through the fence. My fingers curled around it. Quietly. Gratefully.

"Tomorrow," she whispered.

My angel girl reappeared the next day. And every day after.
Always watching, waiting, tossing. Always an apple.

My angel girl and I rarely spoke. I knew nothing about her
except that she was a kind, brave farm girl. What was her name?
Why was she risking her life for me?

The war dragged on. Day after day. Month after month. The work camp filled with sickness
and starvation. But my angel girl sustained me with food. My angel girl filled me with hope.

At long last, the war ended. Many had died, but I was alive. Liberated. Free.

I went to the fence one last time. She was there waiting. "You were my angel girl," I said through the barbed wire.

I saw a tear. A tear in the eye of my angel girl.

After the war, I went with my brothers to England.

I was free from the work camp but a prisoner of the past. Images filled my brain.
The war. The camp. Mama. My old life. My angel girl.

I worked, read, studied. I spent years trying to find ways to leave
the past behind.

When I became a young man, I left for a new life in America.

I arrived in New York. Everything new, unfamiliar.
Memories of my old life wrapped themselves around me.
Squeezed me tight. I thought often of what I had
loved and lost.

I thought often of Mama.

One night, she came to me in a dream. The same dream
I had had years before in the work camp.

"Don't worry, Herman." Mama's soft voice soothed me.
"An angel will save you."

Two days later, a friend invited me out on a double date.

"You will like this girl," he said in the car on the way to dinner.

I did like her. A nurse. Kind. Smart. Green eyes full of life.
Something about them was familiar to me.

She said her name was Roma. She talked of the past and of her life
during the war. A farm. Papers to hide her family's identity.
A small village in Germany.

I knew that village. "I was a prisoner in a work camp there,"
I told Roma.

"I took apples to a boy in that camp." Roma told me how she went
to the fence day after day, month after month.

I thought of the tall, skinny boy in the camp that I had once been.
I thought of my mother, who promised an angel would save me.
Could this be my angel girl from long ago?

After dinner, Roma and I walked along the boardwalk. Sand. Surf.
Setting sun. I had to know if she was the one. Tentative. Afraid. Hopeful. I asked.

"Roma . . . the boy that you took the apples to . . . were the boy's last words,
'*You were my angel girl*'?"

Roma smiled. As I looked into her eyes, I saw a tear.

"You are my angel girl," I said softly to Roma. "And I am your boy."

Before the horrors of World War II set in, Herman Rosenblat lived a happy life with his family in Poland. In August of 1942, Jews from his village were sent away by the Nazis. Women, children, the sick, and the elderly had to go to death camps. Strong, young men were forced to work. Although Herman was only eleven at the time, his mother told him to say he was sixteen. She helped save his life, though she knew it would be the last time she would ever see her son.

Herman Rosenblat with his parents,
1936, Bydgoszcz, Poland

Herman and Roma Rosenblat
at their home in Florida

Herman met Roma during the war when he was assigned to a work camp in a small village in Germany. Roma and her family lived on a farm nearby. They had papers that hid their Jewish identity. When Roma saw Herman through the fence, she knew she had to save him from what would surely be death by starvation. Roma risked her life and the safety of her family to help Herman. Although she saved his life, they never saw each other again until years later when they met on a blind date in New York. Herman and Roma married soon after. They have two children and three grandchildren, and are proud to have celebrated their 50th wedding anniversary. Herman still calls Roma his angel girl.